The Truth About Ruth
and other stories in rhyme

• The Bible in Rhyme •

Andrew Bianchi

Illustrated by Toni Goffe

Abingdon Press

For
Daniel, Rebecca and Amy

Copyright © 2000 John Hunt Publishing Ltd
Text copyright © 2000 Andrew Bianchi
Illustrations copyright © Toni Goffe

Published in the Unites States of America by Abingdon Press,
201 Eighth Avenue South, Nashville, Tennessee 37202

ISBN 0-687-08345-1

Designed and produced by Tony Cantale Graphics

All rights reserved. Except for brief quotations in critical articles or reviews, no part of this book may be reproduced in any manner without prior written permission from the publishers.

Write to: John Hunt Publishing Ltd, 46a West Street, Alresford, Hampshire SO24 9AU, UK.

The rights of Andrew Bianchi and Toni Goffe to be identified as the author and illustrator respectively of this work have been asserted by them in accordance with the Copyright, Designs and Patents Act 1988.

Manufactured in Hong Kong, China

These Bible heroes known from old
Their lives in verse for you unfold:

Gideon Versus Midian
Page 4

The Truth About Ruth
Page 9

Brave Dave and the Defiant Giant
Page 15

Jonah the Moaner
Page 20

Gideon versus Midian

One day while threshing on a rock
  Young Gideon had a dreadful shock:
An angel down from heaven popped
  And right before the fellow stopped.

Without a pleasant, "How d'you do?"
  He said, "Great warrior, God's with you!"
"With us?" replied the startled lad,
  "I think you must be raving mad!

"The Midianites squat on our land
  And pinch the livestock from our hand.
We know God helped us in the past,
  But now it seems we are stuck fast.

"Although I won't His name besmirch
　　I think He's left us in the lurch."
(Despite his dig against the Lord
　　This last remark it was ignored.)

"I'm sending you. Go show some beef!
　　And from your foe, you'll have relief."
"But Lord, I'm such a wimpish worm,"
　　Said Gideon with a cowardly squirm.

"Don't worry son, the two of us
　　Will whack the rotters without fuss."
Now though these fighting words weren't minced,
　　Poor Gideon wasn't quite convinced.

　　　　"I think I'd like a sign or two,
　　　　　　To show me what you say is true.
　　　　Did I say two? Well, even three
　　　　　　Might help my incredulity."

　　　　"Fetch bread and meat (that's off the bone)
　　　　　　And plonk them on that slab of stone."
　　　　Then having done as God had spoke,
　　　　　　The jolly lot went up in smoke.

　　　　　　Later the doubting Gideon cried,
　　　　　　　　"If you will save, as you've implied,
　　　　　　And Israel from these cads release,
　　　　　　　　Perform a number with this fleece.

"If left upon the floor, like so
    Can it be soaked with H_2O,
While when tomorrow I come by
    The land on which it lies is dry?"

And sure enough when past he jogged
    The ex-sheep's coat was waterlogged.
But still his mind was not at rest,
    So he arranged another test.

"Tonight can you change things around
    So when the skin is on the ground
And morning light comes into view
    Only the grass is seeped in dew?"

At sunrise, yes, of course you've guessed
    God had performed the man's request.
Doubts thus removed, young Gideon jumped
    To see the opposition thumped.

Before the fight he heard God state,
    "Your army's size is much too great.
All those with knocking, trembling knees
    Can go and join their families."

Loads beetled off, ten thousand stayed.
  "That's still too many, I'm afraid.
Now listen up to what I think:
  Instruct the men to have a drink,

"Each one who laps like man's best friend
  I'll shortly into battle send,
While those who kneel upon the ground
  Will soon be travelling homeward bound."

Now there were but three hundred left;
  Once more poor Gideon felt bereft.
Said God, "Sneak to the other side."
  So with a mate he went and spied,

And just as soon as they got there
  Something was said that pleased the pair:
A soldier whispered to a friend,
  "I think I'm going round the bend,

"I dreamt our tents were overrun
  By an enormous barley bun."
His pal responded with a fright,
  "It's Gideon the Israelite!"

And so with brimming confidence
  The couple raced back to their tents;
"Get up and quickly follow me –
  The Lord will give us victory."

He split the soldiers in three groups
    Then gave these orders to the troops:
"Take trumpets, torches, empty jars,
    The Midianites will soon be ours!"

Quietly they slithered to the foe.
    "OK," said Gideon, "now blow!
Cry out, 'A weapon for the Lord!
    For Gideon a hacking sword.'"

The trumpets played, the jars were smashed,
    Bright lights from all the torches flashed.
The Israelites watched on amazed
    To see the enemy so fazed.

They turned their heels and swiftly fled,
    At least the ones that were not dead.
For in the general seething scrum
    Each one began to kill his chum.

And so it was that feeble chicken
    Gave all the Midianites a lickin':
The man who'd used that fleece too fully
    Emerged as neither wet, nor woolly!

The Truth About Ruth

When famine struck the promised land
  And stomachs rumbled à la grand,
Elimelech, his sons and wife,
  Left Judah for a tastier life.

And though they all were better fed
  The poor man soon was lying dead.
What's worse, after their wedding day
  His sons both promptly passed away.

The wife, Naomi, had enough.
  Sadly she packed up all her stuff.
"It's time to go back home," she felt,
  "After this rotten hand luck's dealt."

Her sons' wives said, "We'll tag along."
   "No, no, my dears, that would be wrong.
Your kindness I appreciate,
   But stay and find another mate."

With blubbing tears one home did trudge,
   And yet the other wouldn't budge.
"Go back," Naomi said once more.
   But Ruth clung to her mom-in-law,

"Don't tell me to depart from you:
   Wherever you go, I'll go too.
Your tribe, your God, all these I'll share.
   Even in death you'll find me there."

After this speech the two of them
   Toddled along to Bethlehem,
Where all the women said, with glee,
   "Well look who's back, it's Naomi!"

When they returned it was harvest,
   So Ruth said with impressive zest,
"Let me go to the fields, perhaps
   I'll find a few forgotten scraps."

And saying that she went to comb
   For grub that she could take back home.
By chance the field she chose to sieve
   Was of a distant relative.

As she was scrounging there, up pops
    Boaz, the owner of the crops.
The sight of Ruth made his heart whirl.
    He asked his workers, "Who's that girl?"

They told him, so armed with the truth
    He calmly sidled up to Ruth.
"Stay here and gather all you need.
    Word's reached me of your kindly deed.

"I know for Naomi you've cared
    In every way your life you've shared.
May the great God of Israel
    For all these acts reward you well.

"And as you pass from sheaf to sheaf
    I'll see that no one gives you grief."
Encouraged by his little spiel,
    Once more Ruth buckled down with zeal.

At night time she turned home again,
    Her arms weighed down by mounds of
        grain.
Naomi said, "Now Ruth, come clean –
    Tell me the place where you did glean?"

And when she had, Naomi uttered,
   "At least we know our bread's well-buttered.
Now my advice to you would be
   Stick close to Boaz's barley."

Good food, a home, Ruth for a friend,
   Naomi's life seemed on the mend.
Yet what she wanted most by far
   Was to become a grandmamma.

And so she conjured up a scheme
   That would help to fulfil her dream.
She said to Ruth, "I have a plan
   To do with Boaz our kinsman.

"Tonight put on some slinky gear
   And splatter perfume by each ear.
Then go and watch the fellow eat,
   And when he sleeps, lie at his feet."

And though it was a strange request,
   Ruth went upstairs and quickly dressed,
And having plastered on make-up
   She went to watch old Boaz sup:

Who, after guzzling went and slept.
    So to his snoring frame she crept.
When he awoke, with shock he froze –
    There was a woman at his toes!

But when he'd conquered his surprise
    A smuggish gleam passed through his eyes.
"I take it as a compliment
    That you should come down to my tent.

"The younger men you didn't chase,
    But picked an older, wrinkled face.
You know I'd like to marry you,
    But first there's something I must do.

"Another dude could be your groom,"
    Said Boaz, with an air of gloom,
"But if he doesn't want a bride
    Then you'll be mine," he said with pride.

"Now off you go, and in a while
    I hope you'll join me down the aisle."
The next day at the local mart
    He saw his rival for Ruth's heart.

"Naomi wants to sell some land,
    And with it comes a widow's hand.
Sadly you are the first in line,
    But should you field and lass decline,

"Then I will surely take my pick –
　　I'll buy the plot and wed the chick!"
The man's reply filled him with joy:
　　"I guess you'll be the happy boy.

"I wouldn't mind the land, for sure,
　　But not another mother-in-law."
So Ruth and Boaz tied the knot,
　　And very soon they'd filled a cot.

Naomi loved the little chap
　　And often placed him on her lap.
At last her broken heart was glad,
　　Once more a male heir she had!

And when the women of the place
　　Observed the grins upon her face,
They said, "Your Ruth has been so good,
　　Achieving more than males could.

"Her son deserves his share of fame
　　For carrying on the family name."
Their words had a prophetic ring:
　　His grandson David reigned as king!

Brave Dave and the Defiant Giant

Saul and his army marched in line
    To go and fight the Philistine.
They pitched their tents upon a hill
    And waited for a chance to kill.

As battles go it was quite dull,
    The only thing to break the lull
Was when Goliath the local champ
    Emerged each day from out his camp.

Gath's warrior was a fearsome sight –
    Just like a giant, but twice the height,
With front and back kept safe by brass,
    He really looked a touch of class.

"I'd like to know if there's a chap
　　Who's not afraid to have a scrap.
If he should win and I'm left dead,
　　Then we'll serve you," is what he said.

"If at the end of the conflict
　　Your fellow's well and truly licked,
Then things will go the other way
　　And you'll do everything we say."

The Israelites were deeply shocked,
　　Hair stood on end and knees they knocked;
For each one knew well in advance
　　Not one of them would stand a chance.

And so it went, day in day out,
　　In vain he waited for his bout.
Each Israelite was far too clever
　　To risk his life in wild endeavour.

Until young Dave, a shepherd lad
　　Delivering parcels for his dad,
Inquired, "Who is that great fat slob?
　　He needs a smack across the gob."

"You're welcome," was the swift reply,
　　"At beating him to have a try.
The king has promised quite a prize
　　To one who cuts him down to size."

So David trundled off to Saul
　　And begged to have the chance to brawl:
"I'll go and give that creep what for,
　　He'll soon be lifeless on the floor."

Said Saul, "You're just a little boy,
　　That thug will treat you like a toy.
I'll not have you in battle flung
　　With one who's fought since he was young."

"When lion or bear have chased my sheep,
　　I've left them lying in a heap.
The Lord who helped me send them packing
　　Will give Goliath a mighty whacking."

"I like to see one full of pluck,
　　And wish to you the best of luck.
My armor plating should give aid
　　When big boy's temper becomes frayed."

"It's much too big, can't move a thing –
   I think I'd much prefer a sling.
I'll pop five stones into my pouch
   And then he'll see that I'm no slouch."

So off he dashed on skipping toe
   To wipe the smile from his foe.
Who could but giggle with delight
   When David came into his sight.

"Good grief," he said, "is this a joke?
   I thought they'd send a bigger bloke.
This squirt will soon be tasting death:
   I'll hardly have to waste my breath."

"I see you've got your spear and sword,
   But I'm a soldier of the Lord.
I do not care what you might say,
   For He's the one who'll win today."

And putting stone into his sling,
   Dave gave it an almighty swing.
The pebble whizzed right through the sky
   And socked Goliath above the eye.

He tottered first this way, then that,
   And landed with a fearful splat.
Then seeing his opponent dead
   David bounced up to chop his head.

To watch their hero die this way
   Filled all his fans with great dismay.
So while they had the upper hand
   Saul's army chased them from the land.

Jonah the Moaner

"Make tracks to Nineveh, my lad,
   I've heard that place is dreadfully bad.
Go preach hellfire and brim and stone,
   Go preach it in a threatening tone."

But when he heard that Holy voice
   Jonah the prophet muffed his choice.
Unwilling to do what God had said,
   He booked a holiday instead.

His brochure said Tarshish was hip,
   So Jonah went and found a ship.
He paid his fare and ran on board
   To try and scarper from the Lord.

But up his sleeve God had a ruse
   To mess up naughty Jonah's cruise:
He sent a wind upon the sea
   That shook the boat quite violently.

The sailors they were terrified
    And to their favorite gods they cried,
But Jonah for some reason thinks,
    "I'll go below for forty winks."

And while he's sleeping like a pup
    The captain comes and wakes him up.
"Get up and pray – your god may save
    And keep us from this watery grave!"

Then, looking for a chap to blame,
    The crew began the lottery game.
Each one a token had to choose
    And Jonah won – or did he lose?

"Tell us the reason for this gale,
    Your god, and from which land you hail.
Your job, your people – please confess
    Why we are in this ghastly mess!"

"I am a Jew, the Lord I serve,"
    Said Jonah with ironic nerve.
The crew replied, with equal wit,
    "What have you done, you stupid twit?"

As they were chatting to the duffer
    The raging sea was getting rougher.
They begged, "Show us if there's a trick
    To stop this storm, and stop it quick."

"I know this business is my fault,
    So if you want these waves to halt,
Then fling me out into the sea,"
    Said Jonah, altruistic'lly.

Instead, they tried to row to land,
    But it was harder than they'd planned.
The swell grew bigger than before:
    They knew they'd never reach the shore.

So, grabbing Jonah by the neck
    They lifted him above the deck,
And praying that God wouldn't care,
    They lobbed him up into the air.

And when he landed with a splash
    The tempest stopped quick as a flash.
The sailors made a sacrifice
    To thank the Lord for being nice.

Now as they praised a God who saves,
    Strange things went on beneath the waves.
Sooner than grant Jonah's death wish
    God had him gobbled by a fish.

And from inside the creature's guts
  Jonah admitted he'd been nuts.
"You've been so good to think of me
  When all I did was try to flee."

After three days of feeling easy
  The fish's tummy went quite queasy.
Raw prophet wasn't all that grand,
  And so he puked him onto land,

Where, as he shed seaweed and slime,
  Jonah heard God a second time,
"To Nineveh, at steady trot –
  I think by now you've learned what's what."

So off he went and in great power
  He pleaded with that rotten shower.
Soon everyone in that vast town
  Became aware their chips were down.

When news came to the king at last,
  He stood right up and called a fast.
"Dress up in ashes and sackcloth:
  That way we might avert God's wrath."

And he was right, the clever chap.
  The citizens escaped mishap,
For when God saw them all repent
  The thunderbolts were never sent.

Jonah, instead of being glad,
    In fact deep down was hopping mad.
"I much prefer a God who's tough,
    Who zaps and whacks and all that stuff.

"Anger and fury I don't mind,
    What makes me sick is when you're kind.
If that's the way you're going to be,
    I wish you'd put an end to me."

And saying that he left the city,
    Sat down and wallowed in self-pity.
With baking sun and boiling sands,
    Buckets of sweat poured from his glands.

And though He knew he'd been a fool,
    God grew a plant to keep him cool.
Jonah was glad until next day
    A God-sent worm chewed it away.

Once more he went into a tizz.
    "That flower was really quite the bizz."
And once more with an angry sigh
    He moaned, "I wish that I could die."

Said God, "You're sorry for that weed?
    But it was me who gave it feed.
I planted it. I made it grow.
    That shrub belonged to me, you know.

"So if I look upon a place
    That used to be a great disgrace,
And choose to act in love not might,
    Remember, Jonah, that's my right."